easy meals with
just 3 ingredients

easy meals with
just 3 ingredients

75 simple step-by-step recipes for delicious everyday dishes

jenny white

southwater

This edition is published by Southwater, an imprint of Anness Publishing Ltd, Hermes House, 88–89 Blackfriars Road, London SE1 8HA; tel. 020 7401 2077; fax 020 7633 9499

www.southwaterbooks.com; www.annesspublishing.com

If you like the images in this book and would like to investigate using them for publishing, promotions or advertising, please visit our website www.practicalpictures.com for more information.

UK distributor: Book Trade Services; tel. 0116 2759086; fax 0116 2759090; uksales@booktradeservices.com; exportsales@booktradeservices.com
North American distributor: National Book Network; tel. 301 459 3366; fax 301 429 5746; www.nbnbooks.com
Australian distributor: Pan Macmillan Australia; tel. 1300 135 113; fax 1300 135 103; customer.service@macmillan.com.au
New Zealand distributor: David Bateman Ltd; tel. (09) 415 7664; fax (09) 415 8892

Publisher: Joanna Lorenz
Editorial Director: Judith Simons
Senior Editor: Susannah Blake
Copy-editors: Bridget Jones and Sally Somers
Photographer: Craig Robertson, with additional images by Gus Filgate
Home Economist: Jenny White
Home Economist's Assistant: Fergul Connolly
Stylist: Helen Trent
Designer: Paul Oakley
Additional Recipes: Joanna Farrow
Production Controller: Claire Rae

ETHICAL TRADING POLICY
Because of our ongoing ecological investment programme, you, as our customer, can have the pleasure and reassurance of knowing that a tree is being cultivated on your behalf to naturally replace the materials used to make the book you are holding. For further information about this scheme, go to www.annesspublishing.com/trees

A CIP catalogue record for this book is available from the British Library.

Previously published as part of a larger volume, *The Three Ingredient Cookbook*

NOTES
Bracketed terms are intended for American readers.

For all recipes, quantities are given in both metric and imperial measures and, where appropriate, measures are also given in standard cups and spoons. Follow one set, but not a mixture, because they are not interchangeable.

Standard spoon and cup measures are level.
1 tsp = 5ml, 1 tbsp = 15ml, 1 cup = 250ml/8fl oz

Australian standard tablespoons are 20ml. Australian readers should use 3 tsp in place of 1 tbsp for measuring small quantities of gelatine, flour, salt etc.

Medium (US large) eggs are used unless otherwise stated.

PUBLISHER'S NOTE
Although the advice and information in this book are believed to be accurate and true at the time of going to press, neither the authors nor the publisher can accept any legal responsibility or liability for any errors or omissions that may have been made nor for any inaccuracies nor for any loss, harm or injury that comes about from following instructions or advice in this book.

Contents

Introduction

Just because a dish includes only a few ingredients, it doesn't mean you need to compromise on taste and enjoyment. Reducing the number of ingredients you use in a dish has many benefits. Not only does it make shopping easier and quicker, it also means spending less time on preparation because there's less measuring, peeling, scrubbing and chopping to be done. It also allows you to really enjoy the flavours of the few ingredients used. Fresh food tastes fantastic, so why not let the flavours of a few truly fabulous ingredients shine through rather than masking them with the taste of other ingredients?

Keeping it quick, keeping it simple

In today's busy world, time is of the essence – and no one ever seems to have enough of it. When you're trying to cram as much as possible into a single day, often the first thing that falls by the wayside is cooking. When you're busy, the last thing you feel like doing is spending an hour in the supermarket shopping for ingredients, then going home and preparing them before finally cooking a meal. The temptation is to grab a ready-prepared meal to heat up when you get home, or to pick up a takeaway – but sometimes, when you've had a hectic day at work or your kids have been running you ragged, what you really want is to sit down and relax with a tasty home-cooked meal. This book is devoted to helping you do just this.

The idea of making a dish that requires a huge list of ingredients can often put you off before you've even started – the shopping and preparation alone seeming like an unmanageable task. But the good news is that cooking doesn't need to be this way. It's incredibly easy to make delicious dishes using just a few simple ingredients – but the key to success lies in the ingredients you choose, and how you prepare and cook them.

Above and opposite: You need only three ingredients to make this fabulous dish of spaghetti with broccoli and spicy chilli. It tastes delicious and can be made in less than 15 minutes.

Using the right ingredients

The recipes in this book combine basic ingredients such as fruit, vegetables, meat, fish, herbs and spices, but they also make good use of ready-made or pre-prepared products such as curry pastes and pastry. Using these convenient products is a great way to save time, both on preparation and shopping, and in many cases the final results are hardly distinguishable from the home-made version. For example, puff pastry is quite time-consuming to make, while the bought varieties are easy to use, give great results and taste delicious.

When buying basic ingredients, always try to buy the freshest, best quality ones you can to get the maximum flavour. Really fresh ingredients also have the benefit of having a higher nutritional content. If you can buy organic produce, do so. The flavour will be better and you will have the knowledge that they do not contain chemical fertilizers and pesticides.

It is also a good idea to buy fruits and vegetables when they're in season. Although most are available all year round, you can really notice the difference between those that have been ripened naturally and those that have been grown out of season. Strawberries may be available in the middle of winter, but when you cut them open they are often white inside with a slightly waxy texture and none of the sweet, juicy, almost perfumed flavour of the summer fruits. There are so many fabulous ingredients at their peak in their own season that you don't have to buy unseasonal ones. Why buy tired-looking asparagus in autumn when there are plenty of mushrooms, squashes and root vegetables around – all of which can be made into a huge number of delicious, varied meals.

When buying pre-prepared or ready-made ingredients such as stocks for soups or custard to make ice cream, try to buy really good-quality, fresh varieties. When an ingredient is playing an intregral part in a dish, it needs to be well flavoured with a good texture and consistency. If you use a less good product with an inferior flavour, it will really show in the final dish. The same is true of flavouring ingredients such as curry pastes and spicy sauces – go for quality every time and you will reap the benefits.

About this book

Whether you're an experienced cook or an absolute beginner, you'll find the recipes in this book will suit you perfectly. There are dishes for a wide range of occasions: delicious breakfasts and brunches to set you up for the day; easy to prepare midday meals, whether you want a warming soup or a light salad; simple suppers to make when time is short and fabulous dishes to cook when you have more time on your hands or if you're entertaining guests. For when you need a sweet treat, there is an entire chapter devoted to simple but sumptuous home-made desserts. No matter what the occasion, how much time you have, how many people you need to feed, or what you're in the mood for – you are sure to find the perfect quick and easy dish within these pages.

Every recipe has an ingredients list of three items or fewer, and the only other things you will need will come from the storecupboard (pantry): oil or butter to cook with and salt and freshly ground black pepper to season the food. In some cases flavoured oils such as garlic-, lemon-, or herb-infused olive oil are used for cooking or drizzling, so it's well worth keeping a small selection of these oils in the storecupboard.

Essential Ingredients

When you're using only three ingredients or fewer to make a dish, each one needs to be a star player. This is a guide to fresh ingredients and what to look for when buying them but also offers suggestions for those useful, everyday ingredients invaluable in every kitchen. Having a well-stocked storecupboard (pantry) is as essential as selecting only the best fresh ingredients. Try to remember to check cupboards regularly and be vigilant about throwing away out of date ingredients and replenishing them with fresh ones, that way the result will always be a satisfying meal full of rich flavour.

Fruit and Vegetables

Used in both sweet and savoury dishes, fruit can be a main ingredient in a dish or a flavouring to complement or enhance the taste of the other ingredients. The many different varieties offer the cook ample opportunity to create fabulous dishes. Used in salads and savoury dishes, vegetables are delicious served as the main ingredient in a side dish, or as a flavouring ingredient within a main dish.

Meat and Poultry

If possible, buy organic meat and poultry. It is better to eat less meat of better quality than a larger quantity of cheaper meat. Animals and birds that have been raised in a good environment and fed on quality feed produce better-tasting meat than mass-reared, unhappy livestock. When you are cooking with only a few ingredients, each one needs to have an excellent flavour and texture.

Dairy Produce

Milk and milk products, such as yogurt, butter and cheese, are widely used in cooking and can add a delicious richness to many sweet and savoury dishes. Strong-tasting cheeses, such as Gorgonzola or Parmesan, can contribute a wonderful texture, but also add real bite to many savoury dishes. Eggs, another versatile dairy product, are perfect for making simple meals such as omelettes or baked eggs.

Herbs

Invaluable in a huge number of sweet and savoury recipes, herbs add flavour, colour and contrast to many dishes. Fresh herbs are widely available and their flavour is superior to that of dried herbs. Many are easy to grow yourself at home – either in the garden or in a pot on the windowsill. You can grow them from seed, or buy them already growing in pots from supermarkets and garden stores.

Fish and Shellfish

When cooking with fish and shellfish always buy really fresh specimens: look for bright-eyed fish with plump flesh and bright, undamaged skin; they should not smell "fishy" but should have a faint aroma of the sea. Good fishmongers will scale, cut and fillet the fish for you. Choose lobsters and crabs that feel heavy for their size. Store fish and shellfish, covered, towards the bottom of the refrigerator, and use within a day of purchase. Classic aromatics for flavouring fish and shellfish include lemon, lime, parsley, dill, fennel and bay leaves.

Spices and Aromatics

These flavourings play an important role when cooking with a limited number of ingredients, adding a warmth and roundness of flavour to simple dishes. It is difficult to have every spice to hand, but a few key spices will be enough to create culinary magic. Black pepper is an essential seasoning and cumin seeds, coriander seeds, dried chillies and ginger are also good basics.

Store spices in airtight jars or containers in a cool, dark place. Buy small quantities that will be used up fairly quickly because flavours diminish with age.

Pulses and Lentils

Dried pulses such as flageolet beans, chickpeas, red kidney beans, cannellini beans and butter (lima) beans have a long shelf-life, but require lengthy preparation: soaking overnight and then long boiling. The canned alternatives just need to be rinsed in cold water, and can then be used in hot dishes or to make salads. Red lentils also have a relatively short cooking time and are ideal for making a quick and tasty Indian-style dhal.

Pasta, Noodles and Rice

These are particularly useful ingredients to keep in the storecupboard (pantry), and can be used as the base of many dishes. Dried pasta keeps for months in an airtight container. There is a wide variety of pasta in all shapes and sizes. Egg noodles, made from wheat flour and eggs, may be thick, medium or thin. Rice noodles are translucent white noodles that make a good alternative to egg noodles, particularly for those on a gluten-free diet. Rice is a versatile grain that can be served as an accompaniment or form the base of sweet and savoury dishes.

Short-cut Ingredients

There are some useful products available that can help you save valuable time in the kitchen. Ingredients such as pastry, custard, frozen fruit, pasta sauces, bags of salad and pizza base mixes are usually pre-prepared in some way, taking the time and effort out of preparation. Other useful short-cut products are store-bought cakes and cookies which can be combined with cream or fruit to create a simple but indulgent dessert.

Other Ingredients

As well as herbs, spices and aromatics, there are a number of basic flavourings that are widely used in both sweet and savoury cooking. Sweet flavourings such as sugar, honey and chocolate are mainly used in sweet dishes, but small quantities are sometimes used to bring out the flavour of savoury dishes. Alcohol can enhance both sweet and savoury dishes. Soy sauce, Worcestershire sauce, mustard and ready-made curry pastes can be used to enhance the taste of savoury ingredients, while tomato purée (paste) can add extra flavour to a tomato sauce.

Oils, Marinades and Dressings

Essential both for cooking and for adding flavour, there are many different types of oil, all of which have their own character and use in the kitchen. Every cook should have a bottle of oil for cooking and oils for drizzling and flavouring. Olive oil has the best and most pronounced flavour and extra virgin olive oil is ideal for making lightly flavoured salad dressings. Good quality olive oil can also be flavoured with herbs, spices and aromatics to make rich-tasting oils that are perfect for drizzling, making dressings and cooking. Try infusing olive oil with herbs, lemon, chilli or garlic for a wealth of different flavours.

Marinades are strong-tasting mixes which are perfect for adding flavour to meat, poultry, fish and vegetables. Most ingredients should be left to marinate for at least 30 minutes.

Freshly made dressings are delicious drizzled over salads, but are also tasty served with cooked vegetables and simply cooked fish, meat and poultry. You can make these dressings a few hours in advance and store them in a sealed container in the refrigerator until ready to use. Give them a quick whisk before drizzling over the food.

Breakfasts and Brunches

NO ONE WANTS THE BOTHER OF LOTS OF INGREDIENTS
AND LENGTHY PREPARATION FOR THEIR FIRST MEAL OF
THE DAY. THIS COLLECTION OF WONDERFULLY SIMPLE,
YET DELICIOUS DISHES HAS BEEN CREATED WITH THAT
IN MIND. WHETHER YOU WANT A HEALTHY, VITAMIN-
PACKED FRUIT SALAD FOR BREAKFAST OR AN
INDULGENT SERVING OF EGGS BENEDICT FOR A LAZY
WEEKEND BRUNCH, YOU'RE SURE TO FIND THE
PERFECT RECIPE TO SET YOU UP FOR THE DAY.

Zingy Papaya, Lime and Ginger Salad

This refreshing, fruity salad makes a lovely light breakfast, perfect for the summer months. Choose really ripe, fragrant papayas for the best flavour.

SERVES FOUR

1 Cut the papaya in half lengthways and scoop out the seeds, using a teaspoon. Using a sharp knife, cut the flesh into thin slices and arrange on a platter.

2 Squeeze the lime juice over the papaya and sprinkle with the sliced stem ginger. Serve immediately.

2 large ripe papayas

juice of 1 fresh lime

2 pieces preserved stem ginger, finely sliced

VARIATION *This refreshing fruit salad is delicious made with other tropical fruit. Try using 2 ripe peeled stoned mangoes in place of the papayas.*

Cantaloupe Melon
with Grilled Strawberries

If strawberries are slightly underripe, sprinkling them with a little sugar
and grilling them will help bring out their flavour.

SERVES FOUR

1 Preheat the grill (broiler) to high. Hull the strawberries and
cut them in half. Arrange the fruit in a single layer, cut side up,
on a baking sheet or in an ovenproof dish and dust with the
icing sugar.

2 Grill (broil) the strawberries for 4–5 minutes, or until the sugar
starts to bubble and turn golden.

3 Meanwhile, scoop out the seeds from the half melon using a
spoon. Using a sharp knife, remove the skin, then cut the flesh
into wedges and arrange on a serving plate with the grilled
strawberries. Serve immediately.

**115g/4oz/1 cup
strawberries**

**15ml/1 tbsp icing
(confectioners') sugar**

¹/₂ cantaloupe melon

Crunchy Oat Cereal

Serve this tasty crunchy cereal simply with milk or, for a real treat, with yogurt and fresh fruit such as raspberries or blueberries.

SERVES SIX

1 Preheat oven to 160°C/325°F/Gas 3. Mix all the ingredients together and spread on to a large baking tray.

2 Bake for 30–35 minutes, or until golden and crunchy. Leave to cool, then break up into clumps and serve.

200g/7oz/1³/₄ cups jumbo rolled oats

150g/5oz/1¹/₄ cups pecan nuts, roughly chopped

90ml/6 tbsp maple syrup

FROM THE STORECUPBOARD

75g/3oz/6 tbsp butter, melted

COOK'S TIPS
• *This crunchy oat cereal will keep in an airtight container for up to two weeks. Store in a cool, dry place.*
• *You can use other types of nuts if you prefer. Try roughly chopped almonds or hazelnuts instead of pecan nuts, or use a mixture.*

Cranachan

This lovely, nutritious breakfast dish is a traditional Scottish recipe, and is delicious served with a generous drizzle of heather honey. It is also absolutely wonderful served with fresh blueberries or blackberries in place of the raspberries.

SERVES FOUR

75g/3oz crunchy oat cereal

600ml/1 pint/2¹/₂ cups Greek (US strained plain) yogurt

250g/9oz/1¹/₃ cups raspberries

1 Preheat the grill (broiler) to high. Spread the oat cereal on a baking sheet and place under the hot grill for 3–4 minutes, stirring regularly. Set aside to cool.

2 When the cereal has cooled completely, fold it into the Greek yogurt, then gently fold in 200g/7oz/generous 1 cup of the raspberries, being careful not to crush the berries too much.

3 Spoon the yogurt mixture into four serving glasses or dishes, top with the remaining raspberries and serve immediately.

Chocolate Brioche Sandwiches

This luxury breakfast sandwich is a bit of a twist on the classic *pain au chocolat* and beats a boring slice of toast any day. The pale green pistachio nuts work really well with the chocolate spread, adding a satisfying crunch as well as a lovely contrast in colour.

SERVES FOUR

1 Toast the brioche slices until golden on both sides. Spread four of the slices thickly with the chocolate spread and sprinkle over the chopped pistachio nuts in an even layer.

2 Place the remaining brioche slices on top of the chocolate and nuts and press down gently. Using a sharp knife, cut the sandwiches in half diagonally and serve immediately.

COOK'S TIP
Brioche is a classic butter-enriched bread from France. It has a wonderful golden colour and slightly sweet taste. It is available in most supermarkets but you can use ordinary white bread if you can't get hold of brioche. Use an uncut loaf rather than a pre-sliced one so that you can cut thick slices.

8 thick brioche bread slices

120ml/8 tbsp chocolate spread

30ml/2 tbsp shelled pistachio nuts, finely chopped

Roast Bananas with Greek Yogurt and Honey

Roasting bananas like this brings out their natural sweetness. If you are watching the calories, use low-fat Greek yogurt and omit the nuts. Use ripe bananas for maximum flavour. You can also cook bananas in this way over a barbecue and serve them as a simple barbecue dessert drizzled with a little honey.

SERVES FOUR

2 ripe bananas, peeled

500ml/17fl oz/2¹/₄ cups Greek (US strained plain) yogurt with honey

30ml/2 tbsp toasted hazelnuts, roughly chopped

1 Preheat the oven to 200°C/400°F Gas 6. Wrap the bananas in foil and bake for 20 minutes. Leave the bananas to cool completely, then unwrap, place in a small bowl and mash roughly with a fork.

2 Pour the yogurt into a large bowl, add the mashed bananas and gently fold them into the yogurt. Sprinkle with the hazelnuts and serve.

Apricot Turnovers

These sweet and succulent pastries are delicious served with a big cup of milky coffee for a late breakfast or mid-morning treat.

SERVES FOUR

1 Preheat the oven to 190°C/375°F/Gas 5. Roll out the pastry on a lightly floured surface to a 25cm/10in square. Using a sharp knife, cut the pastry into four 13cm/5in squares.

2 Place a tablespoon of the apricot conserve in the middle of each square of pastry. Using a pastry brush, brush the edges of the pastry with a little cold water and fold each square over to form a triangle. Gently press the edges together to seal.

3 Carefully transfer the turnovers to a baking sheet and bake for 15–20 minutes, or until risen and golden. Using a metal spatula, remove the pastries to a wire rack to cool, then dust generously with icing sugar and serve.

225g/8oz ready-made puff pastry, thawed if frozen

60ml/4 tbsp apricot conserve

30ml/2 tbsp icing (confectioners') sugar

Warm Pancakes with Caramelized Pears

If you can find them, use Williams pears for this recipe because they are juicier than most other varieties. For a really indulgent breakfast, top with a generous spoonful of crème fraîche or fromage frais.

SERVES FOUR

8 ready-made pancakes

4 ripe pears, peeled, cored and thickly sliced

30ml/2 tbsp light muscovado (brown) sugar

FROM THE STORECUPBOARD

50g/2oz/¹/₄ cup butter

1 Preheat the oven to 150°C/330°F/Gas 2. Tightly wrap the pancakes in foil and place in the oven to warm through.

2 Meanwhile, heat the butter in a large frying pan and add the pears. Fry for 2–3 minutes, until the undersides are golden. Turn the pears over and sprinkle with sugar. Cook for a further 2–3 minutes, or until the sugar dissolves and the pan juices become sticky.

3 Remove the pancakes from the oven and take them out of the foil. Divide the pears among the pancakes, placing them in one quarter. Fold each pancake in half over the filling, then into quarters and place two folded pancakes on each plate. Drizzle over any remaining juices and serve immediately.

Eggy Bread Panettone

Thickly sliced stale white bread is usually used for eggy bread, but the slightly dry texture of panettone makes a great alternative. Serve with a selection of fresh summer fruits such as strawberries, raspberries and blackcurrants.

SERVES FOUR

2 large (US extra large) eggs

4 large panettone slices

30ml/2 tbsp caster (superfine) sugar

FROM THE STORECUPBOARD

50g/2oz/¹/₄ cup butter or 30ml/2 tbsp sunflower oil

1 Break the eggs into a bowl and beat with a fork, then tip them into a shallow dish. Dip the panettone slices in the beaten egg, turning them to coat evenly.

2 Heat the butter or oil in a large non-stick frying pan and add the panettone slices. (You will probably have to do this in batches, depending on the size of the pan.) Fry the panettone slices over a medium heat for 2–3 minutes on each side, until golden brown.

3 Remove the panettone slices from the pan and drain on kitchen paper. Cut the slices in half diagonally and dust with the sugar. Serve immediately.

Scotch Pancakes with Bacon and Maple Syrup

Also known as drop scones, Scotch pancakes are available in most supermarkets. Raisin varieties also work well in this recipe.

SERVES FOUR

8 ready-made Scotch pancakes

8 dry-cured smoked back (lean) bacon rashers (strips)

30ml/2 tbsp maple syrup

1 Preheat the oven to 150°C/330°F/Gas 2. Wrap the pancakes in a sheet of foil and place them in the oven to warm through.

2 Meanwhile, preheat the grill (broiler) and arrange the bacon on a grill pan. Grill (broil) for 3–4 minutes on each side, until crisp.

3 Divide the warmed pancakes between four warmed serving plates and top with the grilled bacon rashers. Drizzle with the maple syrup and serve immediately.

Croque-monsieur

This classic French toastie is delicious served at any time of day, but with a foaming cup of milky coffee it makes a particularly enjoyable brunch dish. Gruyère is traditionally used, but you could use mild Cheddar instead. Prosciutto and Gorgonzola, served with a smear of mustard, also make a fabulous alternative to the classic ham and Gruyère combination.

SERVES FOUR

8 white bread slices

4 large lean ham slices

175g/6oz Gruyère cheese, thinly sliced

FROM THE STORECUPBOARD

a little softened butter

ground black pepper

1 Preheat the grill (broiler). Arrange the bread on the grill rack and toast four slices on both sides and the other four slices on one side only.

2 Butter the slices of bread that have been toasted on both sides and top with the ham, then the cheese, and season with plenty of ground black pepper.

3 Lay the remaining, half-toasted bread slices on top of the cheese, with the untoasted side uppermost. Grill the tops of the sandwiches until golden brown, then cut them in half using a sharp knife and serve immediately.

Eggs Benedict

Use a good quality bought hollandaise sauce for this recipe because it will make all the difference to the end result. Eggs Benedict are delicious served on half a toasted English muffin. Always use organic eggs – they have a superior flavour to eggs from battery hens.

SERVES FOUR

1 Pour cold water into a medium pan to a depth of about 5cm/2in and bring to a gentle simmer. Crack two eggs into the pan and bring back to the simmer. Simmer for 2–3 minutes, until the white is set, but the yolk is still soft.

2 Meanwhile, arrange the ham slices on four serving plates (or on top of four toasted, buttered muffin halves if using). Remove the eggs from the pan using a slotted spoon and place on top of the ham on two of the plates. Cook the remaining eggs in the same way.

3 Spoon the hollandaise sauce over the eggs, sprinkle with salt and pepper and serve immediately.

4 large (US extra large) eggs

4 lean ham slices

60ml/4 tbsp hollandaise sauce

FROM THE STORECUPBOARD

salt and ground black pepper

VARIATION *If you prefer eggs cooked all the way through, scramble them instead of poaching. Then spoon over the ham and top with hollandaise sauce as before.*

Smoked Salmon and Chive Omelette

The addition of a generous portion of chopped smoked salmon gives a really luxurious finish to this simple, classic dish. You can use this omelette recipe as the basis of endless variations. Simply replace the salmon and chives with other ingredients such as chopped ham and parsley or grated Cheddar and torn basil leaves.

SERVES TWO

1 Beat the eggs until just combined, then stir in the chives and season with salt and pepper.

2 Heat the butter in a medium-sized frying pan until foamy. Pour in the eggs and cook over a medium heat for 3–4 minutes, drawing the cooked egg from around the edge into the centre of the pan from time to time.

3 At this stage, you can either leave the top of the omelette slightly soft or finish it off under the grill (broiler), depending on how you like your omelette. Top with the smoked salmon, fold the omelette over and cut in half to serve.

4 eggs

15ml/1 tbsp chopped fresh chives

50g/2oz smoked salmon, roughly chopped

FROM THE STORECUPBOARD

a knob (pat) of butter

salt and ground black pepper

Quick Kedgeree

Kedgeree is a rice, lentil and onion dish that originally came from India. Fish and eggs were added by the British to make the breakfast dish we know and love today. A garnish of fresh coriander (cilantro) leaves adds extra flavour and colour.

SERVES FOUR

175g/6oz undyed smoked haddock fillet

4 eggs

2 × 250g/9oz packets microwave pilau rice

FROM THE STORECUPBOARD

salt and ground black pepper

1 Preheat the grill (broiler) to medium. Place the smoked haddock on a baking sheet and grill for about 10 minutes, or until cooked through.

2 Meanwhile, place the eggs in a pan of cold water and bring to the boil. Cook for 6–7 minutes, then drain and place under cold running water until cool enough to handle.

3 While the eggs and haddock are cooking, cook the rice according to the instructions on the packet. Shell the eggs and cut into halves or quarters. Flake the fish and gently mix into the rice, with the eggs, taking care not to break up the eggs too much. Spoon onto serving plates, and serve immediately.

Midday Meals

WHAT COULD BE BETTER THAN A TASTY MEAL IN THE
MIDDLE OF THE DAY THAT HAS TAKEN ONLY MOMENTS
TO PREPARE AND NEEDS JUST THREE INGREDIENTS?
WHATEVER YOU'RE IN THE MOOD FOR, WHETHER IT'S
A WARMING BOWL OF SOUP, A HEALTHY SALAD, A
GOURMET SANDWICH OR A BOWL OF PASTA – THERE'S
SOMETHING HERE FOR EVERYONE. THE RECIPES ARE
ALL SO SIMPLE THAT YOU CAN EASILY REDUCE OR
INCREASE THE PROPORTIONS TO MAKE A QUICK LUNCH
FOR ONE, OR A HEALTHY MEAL FOR THE WHOLE FAMILY.

Curried Cauliflower Soup

This spicy, creamy soup is perfect for lunch on a cold winter's day served with crusty bread and garnished with fresh coriander (cilantro). You can also make broccoli soup in the same way, using the same weight of broccoli in place of the cauliflower.

SERVES FOUR

750ml/1¼ pints/3 cups milk

1 large cauliflower

15ml/1 tbsp garam masala

FROM THE STORECUPBOARD

salt and ground black pepper

1 Pour the milk into a large pan and place over a medium heat. Cut the cauliflower into florets and add to the milk with the garam masala and season with salt and pepper.

2 Bring the milk to the boil, then reduce the heat, partially cover the pan with a lid and simmer for about 20 minutes, or until the cauliflower is tender.

3 Let the mixture cool for a few minutes, then transfer to a food processor and process until smooth (you may have to do this in two batches). Return the purée to the pan and heat through gently, checking and adjusting the seasoning, and serve immediately.

Tuscan Bean Soup

Cavolo nero is a very dark green cabbage with a nutty flavour from Tuscany and southern Italy. It is ideal for this traditional recipe. It is available in most large supermarkets, but if you can't get it, use Savoy cabbage instead. Serve with ciabatta bread.

SERVES FOUR

2 x 400g/14oz cans chopped tomatoes with herbs

250g/9oz cavolo nero leaves

400g/14oz can cannellini beans

FROM THE STORECUPBOARD

60ml/4 tbsp extra virgin olive oil

salt and ground black pepper

1 Pour the tomatoes into a large pan and add a can of cold water. Season with salt and pepper and bring to the boil, then reduce the heat to a simmer.

2 Roughly shred the cabbage leaves and add them to the pan. Partially cover the pan and simmer gently for about 15 minutes, or until the cabbage is tender.

3 Drain and rinse the cannellini beans, add to the pan and warm through for a few minutes. Check and adjust the seasoning, then ladle the soup into bowls and drizzle each one with a little olive oil and serve.

Pea Soup with Garlic

If you keep peas in the freezer, you can rustle up this delicious soup in minutes. It has a wonderfully sweet taste and smooth texture and is great served with crusty bread and garnished with mint.

SERVES FOUR

1 garlic clove, crushed

900g/2lb/8 cups frozen peas

1.2 litres/2 pints/5 cups chicken stock

FROM THE STORECUPBOARD

25g/1oz/2 tbsp butter

salt and ground black pepper

1 Heat the butter in a large pan and add the garlic. Fry gently for 2–3 minutes, until softened, then add the peas. Cook for 1–2 minutes more, then pour in the stock.

2 Bring the soup to the boil, then reduce the heat to a simmer. Cover the pan and cook for 5–6 minutes, until the peas are tender. Leave to cool slightly, then transfer the mixture to a food processor and process or until smooth (you may have to do this in two batches).

3 Return the soup to the pan and heat through gently. Season with salt and pepper.

Pea and Mint Omelette

Serve this deliciously light omelette with crusty bread and a green salad for a fresh and tasty lunch. If you're making the omelette for a summer lunch when peas are in season, use freshly shelled peas instead of frozen ones.

SERVES TWO

1 Cook the peas in a large pan of salted boiling water for 3–4 minutes until tender. Drain well and set aside. Break the eggs into a large bowl and beat with a fork. Season well with salt and pepper, then stir in the peas and chopped mint.

2 Heat the butter in a medium frying pan until foamy. Pour in the egg mixture and cook over a medium heat for 3–4 minutes, drawing in the cooked egg from the edges from time to time, until the mixture is nearly set.

3 Finish off cooking the omelette under a hot grill (broiler) until set and golden. Carefully fold the omelette over, cut it in half and serve immediately.

50g/2oz/¹/₂ cup frozen peas

4 eggs

30ml/2 tbsp chopped fresh mint

FROM THE STORECUPBOARD

a knob (pat) of butter

salt and ground black pepper

Seared Tuna Niçoise

A traditional tuna Niçoise consists of tuna, olives, green beans, potatoes and eggs, but this modern version using fresh tuna is a simplified one – although just as tasty. Serve it with a green salad.

SERVES FOUR

1 Put the tuna steaks in a shallow non-metallic dish. Mix the oil and vinegar together and season with salt and pepper.

2 Pour the mixture over the tuna steaks and turn them to coat in the marinade. Cover and chill for up to 1 hour.

3 Heat a griddle pan until smoking hot. Remove the tuna steaks from the marinade and lay them on the griddle pan. Cook for 2–3 minutes on each side, so that they are still pink in the centre. Remove from the pan and set aside.

4 Meanwhile, cook the eggs in a pan of boiling water for 5–6 minutes, then cool under cold running water. Shell the eggs and cut in half lengthways.

5 Pour the marinade on to the griddle pan and cook until it starts to bubble. Divide the tuna steaks among four serving plates and top each with half an egg. Drizzle the marinade over the top and serve immediately.

4 tuna steaks, about 150g/5oz each

30ml/2 tbsp sherry vinegar

2 eggs

FROM THE STORECUPBOARD

45ml/3 tbsp garlic-infused olive oil

salt and ground black pepper

Creamy Parmesan-Baked Eggs

These eggs are delicious as they are but can easily be "dressed up" with additional ingredients. Try adding chopped smoked ham and parsley before you cook them. Serve with thinly sliced bread and butter.

SERVES TWO

1 Preheat the oven to 160°C/325°F/Gas 3. Break the eggs into four ramekin dishes and spoon the cream over the top. Season with salt and ground black pepper and sprinkle the Parmesan cheese on top.

2 Bake the eggs for about 10 minutes, or until they are just set, and serve immediately.

4 large (US extra large) eggs

60ml/4 tbsp double (heavy) cream

30ml/2 tbsp freshly grated Parmesan cheese

FROM THE STORECUPBOARD

salt and ground black pepper

COOK'S TIPS

• *Serve these rich and creamy eggs with a leafy green salad flavoured with fresh tarragon.*
• *For the best results, be sure to serve the eggs as soon as they are cooked.*

Grilled Aubergine, Mint and Couscous Salad

Packets of flavoured couscous are available in most supermarkets – you can use whichever you like, but garlic and coriander is particularly good for this recipe. Serve with a crisp green salad.

SERVES TWO

1 large aubergine (eggplant)

115g/4oz packet garlic-and-coriander (cilantro) flavoured couscous

30ml/2 tbsp chopped fresh mint

FROM THE STORECUPBOARD

30ml/2 tbsp olive oil

salt and ground black pepper

1 Preheat the grill (broiler) to high. Cut the aubergine into large chunky pieces and toss them with the olive oil. Season with salt and pepper to taste and spread the aubergine pieces on a non-stick baking sheet. Grill for 5–6 minutes, turning occasionally, until golden brown.

2 Meanwhile, prepare the couscous according to the instructions on the packet. Stir the grilled aubergine and chopped mint into the couscous, toss thoroughly and serve immediately.

Marinated Courgette and Flageolet Bean Salad

Serve this healthy salad as a light lunch or as an accompaniment to meat and chicken dishes. It has a wonderful bright green colour and is perfect for a summer lunch.

SERVES FOUR

2 courgettes (zucchini), halved lengthways and sliced

400g/14oz can flageolet beans, drained and rinsed

grated rind and juice of 1 unwaxed lemon

FROM THE STORECUPBOARD

45ml/3 tbsp garlic-infused olive oil

salt and ground black pepper

1 Cook the courgettes in boiling salted water for 2–3 minutes, or until just tender. Drain well and refresh under cold running water.

2 Transfer the drained courgettes into a bowl with the beans and stir in the oil, lemon rind and juice and some salt and pepper. Chill for 30 minutes before serving.

VARIATION To add extra flavour to the salad add 30ml/2 tbsp chopped fresh herbs before chilling. Basil and mint both have fresh, distinctive flavours that will work very well.

Roasted Pepper and Hummus Wrap

Wraps make a tasty change to sandwiches and have the bonus that they can be made a few hours in advance without going soggy in the way that bread sandwiches often can. You can introduce all kinds of variation to this basic combination. Try using roasted aubergine (eggplant) in place of the red peppers, or guacamole in place of the hummus. As well as plain flour tortillas, you can also buy flavoured tortillas from most supermarkets.

SERVES TWO

1 large red (bell) pepper, halved and seeded

4 tbsp hummus

2 soft flour tortillas

FROM THE STORECUPBOARD

15ml/1 tbsp olive oil

salt and ground black pepper

1 Preheat the grill (broiler) to high. Brush the pepper halves with the oil and place cut side down on a baking sheet. Grill for 5 minutes, until charred. Put the pepper halves in a sealed plastic bag and leave to cool.

2 When cooled, remove the peppers from the bag and carefully peel away the charred skin and discard. Thinly slice the flesh using a sharp knife.

3 Spread the hummus over the tortillas in a thin, even layer and top with the roasted pepper slices. Season with salt and plenty of ground black pepper, then roll them up and cut in half to serve.

Focaccia with Sardines and Roast Tomatoes

Fresh sardines not only have a lovely flavour and texture, but they are also cheap to buy – so make an economical yet utterly delicious lunch.

SERVES FOUR

1 Preheat the oven to 190°C/375°F/Gas 5. Put the cherry tomatoes in a small roasting pan and drizzle 30ml/2 tbsp of the oil over the top. Season with salt and pepper and roast for 10–15 minutes, or until tender and slightly charred. Remove from the oven and set aside.

2 Preheat the grill (broiler) to high. Brush the sardine fillets with the remaining oil and lay them on a baking sheet. Grill for 4–5 minutes on each side, until cooked through.

3 Split the focaccia in half horizontally and cut each piece in half to give four equal pieces. Toast the cut side under the grill until golden. Top with the sardines and tomatoes and an extra drizzle of oil. Season with black pepper then serve.

20 cherry tomatoes

12 fresh sardine fillets

1 focaccia loaf

FROM THE STORECUPBOARD

45ml/3 tbsp herb-infused olive oil

salt and ground black pepper

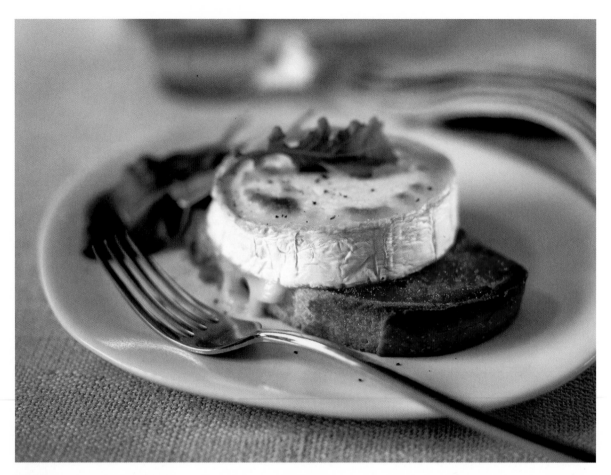

Toasted Sourdough with Goat's Cheese

Choose a good quality, firm goat's cheese for this recipe because it needs to keep its shape during cooking. Serve with fresh rocket leaves.

SERVES TWO

2 thick sourdough bread slices

30ml/2 tbsp chilli jam

2 firm goat's cheese slices, about 90g/3½oz each

FROM THE STORECUPBOARD

30ml/2 tbsp garlic-infused olive oil

ground black pepper

1 Preheat the grill (broiler) to high. Brush the sourdough bread on both sides with the oil, and grill (broil) one side until golden. Spread the un-toasted side of each slice with the chilli jam and top with the goat's cheese.

2 Return the bread to the grill and cook for 3–4 minutes, or until the cheese is beginning to melt and turn golden and bubbling. Season with ground black pepper and serve immediately with rocket (arugula) leaves.

Steak and Blue Cheese Sandwiches

Many people like their rib eye steaks cooked quite rare in the centre, but how you like yours is up to you. Add a couple of minutes to the cooking time if you prefer them more well done.

SERVES TWO

1 Bake the ciabatta according to the instructions on the packet. Remove from the oven and leave to rest for a few minutes. Cut the loaf in half and split each half horizontally.

2 Heat a griddle pan until hot. Brush the steaks with the olive oil and lay them on the griddle pan. Cook for 2–3 minutes on each side, depending on the thickness of the steaks.

3 Remove the steaks from the pan and set aside to rest for a few minutes. Cut them in half and place in the sandwiches with the cheese. Season with salt and pepper, and serve.

1 ready-to-bake ciabatta bread

2 rib eye steaks, about 200g/7oz each

115g/4oz Gorgonzola cheese, sliced

FROM THE STORECUPBOARD

15ml/1 tbsp olive oil

salt and ground black pepper

Warm Penne with Fresh Tomatoes and Basil

This dish is fresh, healthy and ready in minutes. It is the perfect way to use up a glut of ripe summer tomatoes.

SERVES FOUR

500g/1¼lb dried penne

5 very ripe plum tomatoes

1 small bunch of fresh basil

FROM THE STORECUPBOARD

60ml/4 tbsp extra virgin olive oil

salt and ground black pepper

1 Cook the pasta in plenty of salted, boiling water according to the instructions on the packet. Meanwhile, roughly chop the tomatoes, pull the basil leaves from their stems and tear up the leaves.

2 Drain the pasta thoroughly and toss with the tomatoes, basil and olive oil. Season with salt and freshly ground black pepper and serve immediately.

COOK'S TIP *If you cannot find ripe tomatoes, roast them to bring out their flavour. Put the tomatoes in a roasting pan, drizzle with oil and roast at 190°C/375°F/ Gas 5 for 20 minutes, then mash roughly.*

Broccoli and Chilli Spaghetti

The contrast between the hot chilli and the mild broccoli is delicious and goes perfectly with spaghetti. To add extra flavour and texture, sprinkle the spaghetti and broccoli with toasted pine nuts and grated or shaved Parmesan cheese just before serving.

SERVES FOUR

350g/12oz dried spaghetti

450g/1lb broccoli, cut into small florets

1 fat red chilli, seeded and finely chopped

FROM THE STORECUPBOARD

150ml/¼ pint/⅔ cup garlic-infused olive oil

salt and ground black pepper

1 Bring a large pan of lightly salted water to the boil. Add the spaghetti and broccoli and cook for 8–10 minutes, until both are tender. Drain thoroughly.

2 Using the back of a fork crush the broccoli roughly, taking care not to mash the spaghetti strands at the same time.

3 Meanwhile, warm the oil and finely chopped chilli in a small pan over a low heat and cook very gently for 5 minutes.

4 Pour the chilli and oil over the spaghetti and broccoli and toss together to combine. Season to taste. Divide between four warmed bowls and serve immediately.

Spicy Chorizo Sausage and Spring Onion Hash

Use up leftover boiled potatoes for this recipe. Fresh chorizo sausages are available from good butchers and Spanish delis.

SERVES FOUR

1 Heat a large frying pan over a medium heat and add the sausages. Cook for 8–10 minutes, turning occasionally, until cooked through. Remove from the pan and set aside.

2 Add the olive oil to the sausage fat in the pan and then add the potatoes. Cook over a low heat for 5–8 minutes, turning occasionally until golden. Meanwhile, cut the sausages into bite-size chunks and add to the pan.

3 Add the spring onions to the pan and cook for a couple more minutes, until they are piping hot. Season with salt and pepper, and serve immediately.

450g/1lb fresh chorizo sausages

450g/1lb cooked potatoes, diced

1 bunch of spring onions (scallions), sliced

FROM THE STORECUPBOARD

15ml/1 tbsp olive oil

salt and ground black pepper

Baked Sweet Potatoes with Leeks and Gorgonzola

This dish tastes wonderful and looks stunning if you buy the beautiful orange-fleshed sweet potatoes.

SERVES FOUR

4 large sweet potatoes, scrubbed

2 large leeks, washed and sliced

115g/4oz Gorgonzola cheese, sliced

FROM THE STORECUPBOARD

30ml/2 tbsp olive oil

salt and ground black pepper

1 Preheat the oven to 190°C/375°F/Gas 5. Dry the sweet potatoes with kitchen paper and rub them all over with 15ml/ 1 tbsp of the oil. Place them on a baking sheet and sprinkle with salt. Bake for 1 hour, or until tender.

2 Meanwhile, heat the remaining oil in a frying pan and add the sliced leeks. Cook for 3–4 minutes, or until softened and just beginning to turn golden.

3 Cut the potatoes in half lengthways and place them cut side up on the baking sheet. Top with the cooked leeks and season.

4 Lay the cheese slices on top and grill (broil) under a hot grill for 2–3 minutes, until the cheese is bubbling. Serve immediately.

Easy Suppers

AFTER A LONG, HARD DAY, THERE'S NOTHING BETTER
THAN COMING HOME TO A DELICIOUS, WARMING
EVENING MEAL. THIS CHAPTER IS FULL OF TEMPTING
IDEAS THAT ARE QUICK AND SIMPLE TO MAKE AND
OFFER ALL THE COMFORT OF A SUPPER THAT HAS
TAKEN HOURS TO PREPARE. TRY GRILLED HAKE WITH
LEMON AND CHILLI, BAKED HONEY MUSTARD CHICKEN,
SIMPLE POTATO GNOCCHI OR MINTY COURGETTE
LINGUINE. EACH DISH IS EASY AND FLAVOURSOME, SO
JUST SIT BACK, RELAX AND UNWIND.

Minty Courgette Linguine

Sweet, mild courgettes and refreshing mint are a great combination and are delicious with pasta. Dried linguine has been used here but you can use any type of pasta you like. Couscous also works well in place of pasta if you prefer.

SERVES FOUR

450g/1lb dried linguine

4 small courgettes (zucchini), sliced

1 small bunch of fresh mint, roughly chopped

FROM THE STORECUPBOARD

75ml/5 tbsp garlic-infused olive oil

salt and ground black pepper

1 Cook the linguine in plenty of salted, boiling water according to the instructions on the packet.

2 Meanwhile, heat 45ml/3 tbsp of the oil in a large frying pan and add the courgettes. Fry for 2–3 minutes, stirring occasionally, until they are tender and golden.

3 Drain the pasta well and toss with the courgettes and chopped mint. Season with salt and pepper, drizzle over the remaining oil and serve immediately.

Pasta with Roast Tomatoes and Goat's Cheese

Roasting tomatoes brings out their flavour and sweetness, which contrasts perfectly with the sharp taste and creamy texture of goat's cheese. Serve with a crisp green salad flavoured with herbs.

SERVES FOUR

8 large ripe tomatoes

450g/1lb any dried pasta shapes

200g/7oz firm goat's cheese, crumbled

FROM THE STORECUPBOARD

60ml/4 tbsp garlic-infused olive oil

salt and ground black pepper

1 Preheat the oven to 190°C/375°F/Gas 5. Place the tomatoes in a roasting pan and drizzle over 30ml/2 tbsp of the oil. Season well with salt and pepper and roast for 20–25 minutes, or until soft and slightly charred.

2 Meanwhile, cook the pasta in plenty of salted, boiling water, according to the instructions on the packet. Drain well and return to the pan.

3 Roughly mash the tomatoes with a fork, and stir the contents of the roasting pan into the pasta. Gently stir in the goat's cheese and the remaining oil and serve.

Linguine with Anchovies and Capers

This is a fantastic storecupboard recipe. Use salted capers if you can find them, as they have a better flavour than the bottled ones, but remember that you need to rinse them thoroughly before using. Be sure to chop the anchovies finely so that they "melt" into the sauce.

SERVES FOUR

450g/1lb dried linguine

8 anchovy fillets, drained

30ml/2 tbsp salted capers, thoroughly rinsed and drained

FROM THE STORECUPBOARD

75ml/5 tbsp garlic-infused olive oil

salt and ground black pepper

1 Cook the linguine in plenty of salted, boiling water according to the instructions on the packet.

2 Meanwhile, finely chop the anchovy fillets and place in a small pan with the oil and some black pepper. Heat very gently for 5 minutes, stirring occasionally, until the anchovies start to disintegrate.

3 Drain the pasta thoroughly and toss with the anchovies, oil and capers. Season with a little salt and plenty of black pepper to taste. Divide between warmed bowls and serve immediately.

Home-made Potato Gnocchi

These classic Italian potato dumplings are very simple to make – it just requires a little patience when it comes to shaping them. Serve them as soon as they are cooked, tossed in melted butter and fresh sage leaves, sprinkled with grated Parmesan cheese and plenty of black pepper. They make a fabulous alternative to pasta.

900g/2lb floury potatoes, cut into large chunks

2 eggs, beaten

150–175g/5–6oz/1¼–1½ cups plain (all-purpose) flour

FROM THE STORECUPBOARD

10ml/2 tsp salt

SERVES TWO

1 Cook the potatoes in salted, boiling water for 15 minutes, until tender. Drain well and return to the pan, set it over a low heat and dry the potatoes for 1–2 minutes.

2 Mash the potatoes until smooth, then gradually stir in the eggs and salt. Work in enough flour to form a soft dough.

3 Break off small pieces of the dough and roll into balls, using floured hands. Press the back of a fork into each ball to make indentations. Repeat until all the dough has been used. Leave the gnocchi to rest for 15–20 minutes before cooking.

4 Bring a large pan of water to a gentle boil. Add the gnocchi, about ten at a time, and cook for 3–4 minutes, or until they float to the surface. Drain thoroughly and serve as soon as all the gnocchi have been cooked.

VARIATION *To make herb-flavoured gnocchi, add 45ml/3 tbsp chopped fresh herbs, such as basil, parsley and sage, to the potato and flour dough and combine well. Serve with butter and grated Parmesan.*

Classic Margherita Pizza

Bought pizza base mixes are a great storecupboard stand-by. A Margherita Pizza makes a lovely simple supper, but of course you can add any extra toppings you like. Prosciutto and rocket (arugula) make a great addition – just add them to the pizza after it is cooked.

SERVES TWO

half a 300g/11oz packet pizza base mix

45ml/3 tbsp ready-made tomato and basil sauce

150g/5oz mozzarella, sliced

FROM THE STORECUPBOARD

15ml/1 tbsp herb-infused olive oil

salt and ground black pepper

1 Make the pizza base mix according to the instructions on the packet. Brush the base with a little of the olive oil and spread over the tomato and basil sauce, not quite to the edges.

2 Arrange the slices of mozzarella on top of the pizza and bake for 25–30 minutes, or until golden.

3 Drizzle the remaining oil on top of the pizza, season with salt and black pepper and serve immediately, garnished with fresh basil leaves.

Cheesy Leek and Couscous Cake

The tangy flavour of sharp Cheddar cheese goes perfectly with the sweet taste of leeks. The cheese melts into the couscous and helps it stick together, making a firm cake that's easy to cut into wedges. Serve with a crisp green salad.

SERVES FOUR

300g/11oz couscous

2 leeks, sliced

200g/7oz mature Cheddar or Monterey Jack, grated

FROM THE STORECUPBOARD

45ml/3 tbsp olive oil

salt and ground black pepper

VARIATION *There are endless variations on this tangy, tasty cake but choose a cheese that melts well because it will help the cake to stick together. Try using caramelized onions and blue cheese in place of the leeks and Cheddar.*

1 Put the couscous in a large heatproof bowl and pour over 450ml/³/₄ pint/scant 2 cups boiling water. Cover and set aside for about 15 minutes, or until all the water has been absorbed.

2 Heat 15ml/1 tbsp of the oil in a 23cm/9in non-stick frying pan. Add the leeks and cook over a medium heat for 4–5 minutes, stirring occasionally, until tender and golden.

3 Remove the leeks with a slotted spoon and stir them into the couscous. Add the grated cheese and some salt and pepper and stir through. Heat the remaining oil in the pan and tip in the couscous and leek mixture. Pat down firmly to form a cake and cook over a fairly gentle heat for 15 minutes, or until the underside is crisp and golden.

4 Slide the couscous cake onto a plate, then invert it back into the pan to cook the other side. Cook for a further 5–8 minutes, or until golden, then remove from the heat. Slide on to a board and serve cut into wedges.

Salt Cod and Potato Fritters

These little fritters are extremely easy to make and taste delicious. Serve them simply with a wedge of fresh lemon and some watercress or green salad. Offer a bowl of garlic mayonnaise for dipping.

MAKES ABOUT TWENTY-FOUR

450g/1lb salt cod fillets

500g/1¼lb floury potatoes, unpeeled

plain (all-purpose) flour, for coating

FROM THE STORECUPBOARD

vegetable oil, for deep-frying

salt and ground black pepper

1 Put the salt cod in a bowl, pour over cold water and leave to soak for 24 hours, changing the water every 6–8 hours. Drain, rinse and place in a pan of cold water. Slowly bring to the boil and simmer for 5 minutes, then drain and cool. When cooled, remove any bones and skin and mash the fish with a fork.

2 Cook the potatoes in their skins in a pan of salted boiling water for 20–25 minutes, or until just tender. Peel and mash.

3 Add the fish to the potatoes and mix well. Season to taste with salt and pepper. Break off walnut-sized pieces of the mixture and roll into balls. Place on a floured plate, cover and chill for 20–30 minutes. Roll each ball lightly in flour, dusting off any excess.

4 Heat enough oil for deep-frying in a large pan and fry the balls for 5–6 minutes, or until golden. Remove with a slotted spoon and drain on kitchen paper. Serve hot or warm.

Asian-style Crab Cakes

You could serve these patties as a simple supper, or an appetizer for eight people. Use a mixture of white and brown crab meat, as the dark adds a depth of flavour and texture. Serve with sweet chilli sauce.

MAKES SIXTEEN

450g/1lb/2²⁄₃ cups fresh crab meat, white and brown

15ml/1 tbsp grated fresh root ginger

15–30ml/1–2 tbsp plain (all-purpose) flour

FROM THE STORECUPBOARD

60ml/4 tbsp sunflower oil

salt and ground black pepper

1 Put the crab meat in a bowl and add the ginger, some salt and ground black pepper and the flour. Stir well until thoroughly mixed.

2 Using floured hands, divide the mixture into 16 equal-sized pieces and shape roughly into patties.

3 Heat the sunflower oil in a frying pan and add the patties, four at a time. Cook for 2–3 minutes on each side, until golden. Remove with a metal spatula and leave to drain on kitchen paper for a few minutes.

4 Keep the cooked crab cakes warm while you cook the remaining patties in the same way. Serve immediately.

Grilled Hake with Lemon and Chilli

Choose firm hake fillets, as thick as possible. This is an ideal recipe if you are counting the calories, because it is low in fat. Serve with new potatoes and steamed fine green beans. Or, if you're not counting calories, serve with creamy mashed potatoes with plenty of butter stirred in.

SERVES FOUR

4 hake fillets, each 150g/5oz

finely grated rind and juice of 1 unwaxed lemon

15ml/1 tbsp crushed chilli flakes

FROM THE STORECUPBOARD

30ml/2 tbsp olive oil

salt and ground black pepper

1 Preheat the grill (broiler) to high. Brush the hake fillets all over with the olive oil and place them skin side up on a baking sheet.

2 Grill (broil) the fish for 4–5 minutes, until the skin is crispy, then carefully turn them over using a metal spatula.

3 Sprinkle the fillets with the lemon rind and chilli flakes and season with salt and ground black pepper.

4 Grill the fillets for a further 2–3 minutes, or until the hake is cooked through. (Test using the point of a sharp knife; the flesh should flake.) Squeeze over the lemon juice just before serving.

Honey Mustard Chicken

Chicken thighs have a rich flavour, but if you want to cut down on fat, use four chicken breast portions instead and cook for 20–25 minutes. Serve with a chunky tomato and red onion salad.

SERVES FOUR

1 Preheat the oven to 190°C/375°F/Gas 5. Put the chicken thighs in a single layer in a roasting pan.

2 Mix together the mustard and honey, season with salt and ground black pepper to taste and brush the mixture all over the chicken thighs.

3 Cook for 25–30 minutes, brushing the chicken with the pan juices occasionally, until cooked through. (To check the chicken is cooked through, skewer it with a sharp knife; the juices should run clear.)

8 chicken thighs

60ml/4 tbsp wholegrain mustard

60ml/4 tbsp clear honey

FROM THE STORECUPBOARD

salt and ground black pepper

Stir-fried Chicken with Thai Basil

Thai basil, sometimes called holy basil, has purple-tinged leaves and a more pronounced, slightly aniseedy flavour than the usual varieties. It is available in most Asian food stores but if you can't find any, use a handful of ordinary basil instead. Serve this fragrant stir-fry with plain steamed rice or boiled noodles and soy sauce on the side.

SERVES FOUR

1 Using a sharp knife, slice the chicken breast portions into strips. Halve the peppers, remove the seeds, then cut each piece of pepper into strips.

2 Heat the oil in a wok or large frying pan. Add the chicken and red peppers and stir-fry over a high heat for about 3 minutes, until the chicken is golden and cooked through. Season with salt and ground black pepper.

3 Roughly tear up the basil leaves, add to the chicken and peppers and toss briefly to combine. Serve immediately.

4 skinless chicken breast fillets, cut into strips

2 red (bell) peppers

1 small bunch of fresh Thai basil

FROM THE STORECUPBOARD

30ml/2 tbsp garlic-infused olive oil

salt and ground black pepper

Crème Fraîche and Coriander Chicken

Boneless chicken thighs are used for this recipe but you can substitute breast portions if you like. Be generous with the coriander leaves, as they have a wonderful fragrant flavour, or use chopped parsley instead. Serve with creamy mashed potatoes. To make a lower fat version of this dish, use chicken breast portions and low-fat crème fraîche.

SERVES FOUR

6 skinless chicken thigh fillets

60ml/4 tbsp crème fraîche

1 small bunch of fresh coriander (cilantro), roughly chopped

FROM THE STORECUPBOARD

15ml/1 tbsp sunflower oil

salt and ground black pepper

1 Cut each chicken thigh into three or four pieces. Heat the oil in a large frying pan, add the chicken and cook for about 6 minutes, turning occasionally, until cooked through.

2 Add the crème fraîche to the pan and stir until melted, then allow to bubble for 1–2 minutes.

3 Add the chopped coriander to the chicken and stir to combine. Season with salt and ground black pepper to taste, and serve immediately.

Fragrant Lemon Grass and Ginger Pork Patties

Lemon grass lends a fragrant citrus flavour to pork, enhanced by the fresh zing of ginger. Serve the patties in burger buns with thick slices of juicy tomato, crisp, refreshing lettuce and a splash of chilli sauce.

SERVES FOUR

450g/1lb/2 cups minced (ground) pork

15ml/1 tbsp fresh root ginger, grated

1 lemon grass stalk

FROM THE STORECUPBOARD

30ml/2 tbsp sunflower oil

salt and ground black pepper

1 Put the pork in a bowl and stir in the ginger. Season with salt and pepper. Remove the tough outer layers from the lemon grass stalk and discard. Chop the centre part as finely as possible and mix into the pork. Shape into four patties and chill for about 20 minutes.

2 Heat the oil in a large, non-stick frying pan and add the patties. Fry for 3–4 minutes on each side over a gentle heat, until cooked through. Remove from the pan with a metal spatula and drain on kitchen paper, then serve.

Pan-fried Gammon with Cider

Gammon and cider are a delicious combination with the sweet, tangy flavour of cider complementing the gammon perfectly. Serve with mustard mashed potatoes.

4 gammon steaks (smoked or cured ham), 225g/8oz each

150ml/¹⁄₄ pint/²⁄₃ cup dry (hard) cider

45ml/3 tbsp double (heavy) cream

FROM THE STORECUPBOARD

30ml/2 tbsp sunflower oil

salt and ground black pepper

SERVES FOUR

1 Heat the oil in a large frying pan until hot. Neatly snip the rind on the gammon steaks to stop them curling up and add them to the pan.

2 Cook the steaks for 3–4 minutes on each side, then pour in the cider. Allow to boil for a couple of minutes, then stir in the cream and cook for 1–2 minutes, or until thickened. Season with salt and pepper, and serve immediately.

Caramelized Onion and Sausage Tarte Tatin

Toulouse sausages have a garlicky flavour and meaty texture that is delicious with fried onions. Serve with a green salad of bitter leaves.

SERVES FOUR

450g/1lb Toulouse sausages

2 large onions, sliced

250g/9oz ready-made puff pastry, thawed if frozen

FROM THE STORECUPBOARD

45ml/3 tbsp sunflower oil

salt and ground black pepper

1 Heat the oil in a 23cm/9in non-stick frying pan with an ovenproof handle, and add the sausages. Cook over a gentle heat, turning occasionally, for 7–10 minutes, or until golden and cooked through. Remove from the pan and set aside.

2 Preheat the oven to 190°C/375°F/Gas 5. Pour the remaining oil into the frying pan and add the onions. Season with salt and pepper and cook over a gentle heat for 10 minutes, stirring occasionally, until caramelized and tender.

3 Slice each sausage into four or five chunks and stir into the onions. Remove from the heat and set aside.

4 Roll out the puff pastry and cut out a circle slightly larger than the frying pan. Lay the pastry over the sausages and onions, tucking the edges in all the way around. Bake for 20 minutes, or until the pastry is risen and golden. Turn out on to a board, pastry side down, cut into wedges and serve.

Marinated Lamb
with Oregano and Basil

Lamb leg steaks are chunky with a sweet flavour and go well with oregano and basil.
However, you could also use finely chopped rosemary or thyme. Serve with couscous.

SERVES FOUR

1 Put the lamb in a shallow, non-metallic dish. Mix 45ml/3 tbsp of the oil with the oregano, basil and some salt and pepper, reserving some of the herbs for garnish. Pour over the lamb and turn to coat in the marinade. Cover and chill for up to 8 hours.

2 Heat the remaining oil in a large frying pan. Remove the lamb from the marinade and fry for 5–6 minutes on each side, until slightly pink in the centre. Add the marinade and cook for 1–2 minutes until warmed through. Garnish with the reserved herbs and serve.

4 large or 8 small lamb leg steaks

1 small bunch of fresh oregano, roughly chopped

1 small bunch of fresh basil, torn

FROM THE STORECUPBOARD

60ml/4 tbsp garlic-infused olive oil

salt and ground black pepper

Take Your Time

THIS CHAPTER IS DEVOTED TO THOSE DELICIOUS
DISHES THAT YOU NEED TO PLAN AHEAD FOR. THEY
MAY REQUIRE LENGTHY PREPARATION OR SLOW
COOKING BUT THEY STILL NEED ONLY THREE MAIN
INGREDIENTS. THERE ARE FABULOUS ROASTS AND
OVEN-BAKED DISHES, SENSATIONAL STEWS AND
WONDERFULLY FLAVOURSOME MARINATED DISHES TO
CHOOSE FROM. ENJOY THEM WHEN YOU'VE GOT TIME
ON YOUR HANDS – FOR A SPECIAL DINNER OR FOR A
LEISURELY SUNDAY LUNCH WITH ALL THE FAMILY.

Oven-baked Porcini Risotto

This risotto is easy to make because you don't have to stand over it stirring constantly as it cooks, as you do with a traditional risotto.

SERVES FOUR

25g/1oz/¹/₂ cup dried porcini mushrooms

1 onion, finely chopped

225g/8oz/generous 1 cup risotto rice

FROM THE STORECUPBOARD

30ml/2 tbsp garlic-infused olive oil

salt and ground black pepper

1 Put the mushrooms in a heatproof bowl and pour over 750ml/1¹/₄ pints/3 cups boiling water. Leave to soak for 30 minutes. Drain the mushrooms through a sieve lined with kitchen paper, reserving the soaking liquor. Rinse the mushrooms thoroughly under running water to remove any grit, and dry on kitchen paper.

2 Preheat the oven to 180°C/350°F/Gas 4. Heat the oil in a roasting pan on the hob and add the onion. Cook for 2–3 minutes, or until softened but not coloured.

3 Add the rice and stir for 1–2 minutes, then add the mushrooms and stir. Pour in the mushroom liquor and mix well. Season with salt and pepper, and cover with foil.

4 Bake in the oven for 30 minutes, stirring occasionally, until all the stock has been absorbed and the rice is tender. Divide between warm serving bowls and serve immediately.

Creamy Red Lentil Dhal

This makes a tasty winter supper for vegetarians and meat eaters alike. Serve with naan bread, coconut cream and fresh coriander (cilantro) leaves. The coconut cream gives this dish a really rich taste.

SERVES FOUR

150g/5oz/²/₃ cup red lentils

15ml/1 tbsp hot curry paste

FROM THE STORECUPBOARD

15ml/1 tbsp sunflower oil

salt and ground black pepper

1 Heat the oil in a large pan and add the lentils. Fry for 1–2 minutes, stirring continuously, then stir in the curry paste and 600ml/1 pint/2¹/₂ cups boiling water.

2 Bring the mixture to the boil, then reduce the heat to a gentle simmer. Cover the pan and cook for 15 minutes, stirring occasionally, until the lentils are tender and the mixture has thickened.

3 Season the dhal with plenty of salt and ground black pepper to taste, and serve piping hot.

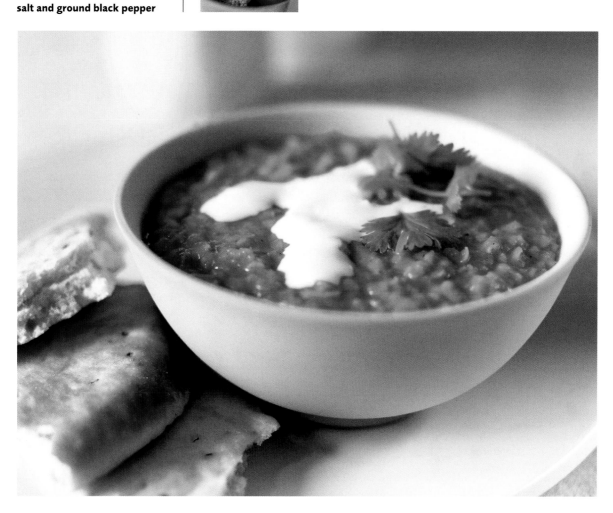

Potato, Pancetta and Parmesan Galette

This richly flavoured "pie" is a perfect winter warmer. A mandolin will make quick work of the potatoes – slicing them thinly – but be careful of your fingers because the blade is sharp.

SERVES FOUR

1 Preheat the oven to 180°C/350°F/Gas 4. Brush a 20cm/8in ovenproof dish with some of the oil. Arrange one-third of the potatoes in the bottom of the dish, season and lay three slices of pancetta over the top. Sprinkle over a little cheese and arrange another layer of potatoes on the top.

2 Lay the remaining pancetta on top of the potatoes and sprinkle with a little more Parmesan and seasoning. Top with the remaining potatoes, season with salt and pepper and drizzle over the remaining olive oil. Press the potatoes down firmly and cover the dish with foil.

3 Bake for 30–35 minutes, then uncover and sprinkle with the remaining Parmesan. Bake for a further 15–20 minutes, or until golden. Leave to rest for about 10 minutes, then cut into wedges to serve.

450g/1lb waxy potatoes, peeled and very thinly sliced

6 pancetta slices

50g/2oz/²/₃ cup freshly grated Parmesan cheese

FROM THE STORECUPBOARD

30ml/2 tbsp garlic-infused olive oil

salt and ground black pepper

Roast Acorn Squash with Spinach and Gorgonzola

Roasting squash brings out its sweetness, here offset by tangy cheese. Acorn squash has been used here, but any type of squash will give delicious results.

SERVES FOUR

4 acorn squash

250g/9oz baby spinach leaves, washed

200g/7oz Gorgonzola cheese, sliced

FROM THE STORECUPBOARD

45ml/3 tbsp garlic-infused olive oil

salt and ground black pepper

1 Preheat the oven to 190°C/375°F/Gas 5. Cut the tops off the squash, and scoop out and discard the seeds. Place the squash, cut side up, in a roasting pan and drizzle with 30ml/ 2 tbsp of the oil. Season with salt and pepper and bake for 30–40 minutes, or until tender.

2 Heat the remaining oil in a large frying pan and add the spinach leaves. Cook over a medium heat for 2–3 minutes, until the leaves are just wilted. Season with salt and pepper and divide between the squash halves.

3 Top with the Gorgonzola and return to the oven for 10 minutes, or until the cheese has melted. Season with ground black pepper and serve.

Teriyaki Salmon

Bottles of teriyaki sauce – a lovely rich Japanese glaze – are available in most large supermarkets and Asian stores. Serve the salmon with sticky rice or soba noodles.

SERVES FOUR

4 salmon fillets, 150g/5oz each

75ml/5 tbsp teriyaki marinade

5cm/2in piece of fresh root ginger, peeled and cut into matchsticks

FROM THE STORECUPBOARD

150ml/¼ pint/⅔ cup sunflower oil

1 Put the salmon in a shallow, non-metallic dish and pour over the teriyaki marinade. Cover and chill for 2 hours.

2 Meanwhile, heat the sunflower oil in a small pan and add the ginger. Fry for 1–2 minutes, or until golden and crisp. Remove with a slotted spoon and drain on kitchen paper.

3 Heat a griddle pan until smoking hot. Remove the salmon from the marinade and add, skin side down, to the pan. Cook for 2–3 minutes, then turn over and cook for a further 1–2 minutes, or until cooked through. Remove from the pan and divide among four serving plates. Top the salmon fillets with the crispy fried ginger.

4 Pour the marinade into the pan and cook for 1–2 minutes. Pour over the salmon and serve.

Roast Mackerel with Spicy Chermoula Paste

Chermoula is a spice mix used widely in Moroccan and North African cooking. It is now readily available in most large supermarkets.

SERVES FOUR

4 whole mackerel, cleaned and gutted

2–3 tbsp chermoula

2 red onions, sliced

FROM THE STORECUPBOARD

75ml/5 tbsp olive oil

salt and freshly ground black pepper

1 Preheat the oven to 190°C/375°F/Gas 5. Place each mackerel on a large sheet of baking parchment. Using a sharp knife, slash each fish several times.

2 In a small bowl, mix the chermoula with the olive oil, and spread over the mackerel, rubbing the mixture into the cuts.

3 Scatter the red onions over the mackerel, and season with salt and pepper. Scrunch the ends of the paper together to seal the fish and place on a baking tray. Bake for 20 minutes, until the mackerel is cooked through. Serve in the paper parcels, to be unwrapped at the table.

Tandoori Chicken

If you have time, prepare this dish when you get up in the morning, so that it's ready to cook for supper. Serve with a red onion and cucumber salad and warmed naan bread.

SERVES FOUR

4 skinless chicken breast fillets and 4 skinless chicken thigh fillets

200ml/7fl oz/scant 1 cup Greek (US strained plain) yogurt

45ml/3 tbsp tandoori curry paste

FROM THE STORECUPBOARD

salt and ground black pepper

1 Using a sharp knife, slash the chicken breasts and thighs and place in a shallow, non-metallic dish.

2 Put the curry paste and yogurt in a bowl and mix together. Season with salt and pepper, then pour over the chicken and toss to coat well. Cover the dish with clear film (plastic wrap) and chill for at least 8 hours.

3 Preheat the oven to 190°C/375°F/Gas 5. Remove the clear film from the chicken and transfer the dish to the oven. Bake for 20–30 minutes, or until the chicken is cooked through. Serve immediately.

Roast Chicken with Black Pudding and Sage

The combination of juicy roast chicken and black pudding is wonderful. Serve as part of a Sunday roast or simply with a salad.

SERVES FOUR

1 medium oven-ready chicken

115g/4oz black pudding (blood sausage), skinned

30ml/2 tbsp fresh sage leaves

FROM THE STORECUPBOARD

25g/1oz/2 tbsp softened butter

salt and ground black pepper

1 Preheat the oven to 190°C/375°F/Gas 5. Carefully push your fingers between the skin and the flesh at the neck end of the bird to loosen it, making sure you don't tear the skin.

2 Shape the black pudding into a flat, roundish shape, to fit the space between the skin and the breast meat. Push it under the skin with half the sage leaves.

3 Smooth the skin back and tuck underneath. Tie the legs together and place the chicken in a roasting pan. Spread the butter over the breast and thighs, and season. Sprinkle over the remaining sage leaves and roast for 1^1/$_2$ hours, or until the chicken is cooked through. Remove to a board and leave to rest for 10 minutes before carving.

Sticky Glazed Pork Ribs

These spare ribs have a lovely sweet-and-sour flavour and are always as popular with children as they are with adults, making them the perfect choice for a family meal. They're also great for cooking over a barbecue; make sure you leave them to marinate for at least 30 minutes before cooking. To enjoy sticky ribs at their best you need to get stuck in and eat them with your fingers, so make sure you serve them with plenty of paper napkins.

SERVES FOUR

1 Preheat the oven to 190°C/375°F/Gas 5. Put the spare ribs in a roasting pan and season well with plenty of salt and ground black pepper.

2 In a small bowl, mix together the honey and soy sauce and pour over the ribs. Turn the ribs several times, spooning over the mixture until thoroughly coated.

3 Bake the spare ribs for 30 minutes, then increase the oven temperature to 220°C/425°F/Gas 7 and cook for a further 10 minutes, or until the honey and soy sauce marinade turns into a thick, sticky glaze.

900g/2lb pork spare ribs

75ml/5 tbsp clear honey

75ml/5 tbsp light soy sauce

FROM THE STORECUPBOARD

salt and ground black pepper

Chinese Spiced Pork Chops

Five-spice powder is a fantastic ingredient for perking up dishes and adding a good depth of flavour. The five different spices – Szechuan pepper, cinnamon, cloves, fennel seeds and star anise – are perfectly balanced, with the aniseed flavour of star anise predominating. Serve the chops with lightly steamed pak choi (bok choy) and plain boiled rice.

SERVES FOUR

4 large pork chops, about 200g/7oz each

15ml/1 tbsp Chinese five-spice powder

30ml/2 tbsp soy sauce

FROM THE STORECUPBOARD

30ml/2 tbsp garlic-infused olive oil

1 Arrange the pork chops in a single layer in a non-metallic roasting pan or baking dish.

2 Sprinkle the five-spice powder over the chops, then drizzle over the soy sauce and garlic infused oil. (Alternatively, mix together the garlic-infused olive oil and five-spice powder, and pour over the chops.)

3 Using your hands, rub the mixture into the meat. Cover the dish with clear film (plastic wrap) and chill for 2 hours.

4 Preheat the oven to 160°C/325°F/Gas 3. Uncover the dish and bake for 30–40 minutes, or until the pork is cooked through and tender. Serve immediately.

Roast Pork with Juniper Berries and Bay

Juniper berries have a strong, pungent taste and are a great flavouring for rich, fatty meats such as pork, while bay leaves add a lovely aroma. Serve with roast potatoes and lightly cooked leafy green vegetables.

SERVES FOUR TO SIX

1kg/2¼lb boned leg of pork

5 fresh bay leaves

6 juniper berries

FROM THE STORECUPBOARD

15ml/1 tbsp olive oil

salt and ground black pepper

1 Preheat the oven to 180°C/350°F/Gas 4. Open out the pork and season with plenty of salt and black pepper.

2 Lay the bay leaves on the pork and sprinkle over the juniper berries. Carefully roll up the pork to enclose the bay leaves and juniper berries and tie with string to secure.

3 Rub the skin with the oil and then rub in plenty of salt. Roast the pork for 20 minutes per 450g/1lb, plus an extra 20 minutes.

4 Remove the pork from the oven and leave to rest for about 10 minutes before carving, then serve immediately.

Lamb Chops with a Mint Jelly Crust

Mint and lamb are classic partners, and the breadcrumbs used here add extra texture. Serve the chops with sweet potatoes baked in their skins and some steamed green vegetables.

SERVES FOUR

1 Preheat the oven to 190ºC/375ºF/Gas 5. Place the lamb chops on a baking sheet and season with plenty of salt and ground black pepper.

2 Put the breadcrumbs and mint jelly in a bowl and mix together to combine. Spoon the breadcrumb mixture on top of the chops, pressing down firmly with the back of a spoon making sure they stick to the chops.

3 Bake the chops for 20–30 minutes, or until they are just cooked through. Serve immediately.

8 lamb chops, about 115g/4oz each

50g/2oz/1 cup fresh white breadcrumbs

30ml/2 tbsp mint jelly

FROM THE STORECUPBOARD

salt and ground black pepper

Roast Shoulder of Lamb with Whole Garlic Cloves

The potatoes catch the lamb fat as it cooks, giving garlicky, juicy results. Return the potatoes to the oven to keep warm while you leave the lamb to rest before carving. Serve with seasonal vegetables.

SERVES FOUR TO SIX

675g/1¹/₂lb waxy potatoes, peeled and cut into large dice

12 garlic cloves, unpeeled

1 whole shoulder of lamb

FROM THE STORECUPBOARD

45ml/3 tbsp olive oil

salt and ground black pepper

1 Preheat the oven to 180°C/350°F/Gas 4. Put the potatoes and garlic cloves into a large roasting pan and season with salt and pepper. Pour over 30ml/2 tbsp of the oil and toss the potatoes and garlic to coat.

2 Place a rack over the roasting pan, so that it is not touching the potatoes. Place the lamb on the rack and drizzle over the remaining oil. Season with salt and pepper.

3 Roast the lamb and potatoes for 2–2¹/₂ hours, or until the lamb is cooked through. Halfway through the cooking time, carefully take the lamb and the rack off the roasting pan and turn the potatoes to ensure even cooking.

Roast Leg of Lamb with Rosemary and Garlic

This is a classic combination of flavours, and always popular. Serve as a traditional Sunday lunch with roast potatoes and vegetables. Leaving the lamb to rest before carving ensures a tender result.

SERVES FOUR TO SIX

1 leg of lamb, approx 1.8kg/4lb

2 garlic cloves, finely sliced

leaves from 2 sprigs of fresh rosemary

FROM THE STORECUPBOARD

30ml/2 tbsp olive oil

salt and ground black pepper

1 Preheat the oven to 190°C/375°F/Gas 5. Using a small sharp knife, make slits at 4cm/1$^{1}/_{2}$in intervals over the lamb, deep enough to hold a piece of garlic. Push the garlic and rosemary leaves into the slits.

2 Drizzle the olive oil over the top of the lamb and season with plenty of salt and ground black pepper. Roast for 25 minutes per 450g/1lb of lamb, plus another 25 minutes.

3 Remove the lamb from the oven and leave to rest for about 15 minutes before carving.

Meatballs in Tomato Sauce

Cook meatballs in their sauce, rather than frying them first, because this helps keep them nice and moist. Serve in the traditional way with spaghetti and shavings of Parmesan cheese.

SERVES FOUR

225g/8oz/1 cup minced (ground) beef

4 Sicilian-style sausages

2 x 400g/14oz cans pomodorino tomatoes

FROM THE STORECUPBOARD

salt and ground black pepper

1 Put the minced beef in a bowl and season with salt and pepper. Remove the sausages from their skins and mix thoroughly into the beef.

2 Shape the mixture into balls about the size of large walnuts and arrange in a single layer in a shallow baking dish. Cover and chill for 30 minutes.

3 Preheat the oven to 180°C/350°F/Gas 4. Process the tomatoes in a food processor until just smooth, and season. Pour over the meatballs, making sure they are all covered.

4 Bake the meatballs for 40 minutes, stirring once or twice until they are cooked through, then serve.

Beef Cooked in Red Wine

Shin of beef is traditionally a quite tough cut that needs long, slow cooking, and marinating the beef in red wine gives a tender result. Sprinkle the stew with rosemary and serve with mashed potatoes.

SERVES FOUR TO SIX

1 Put the beef in a casserole dish with the garlic and some black pepper, and pour over the red wine. Stir to combine, then cover and chill for at least 12 hours.

2 Preheat the oven to 160°C/325°F/Gas 3. Cover the casserole with a tight-fitting lid and transfer to the oven. Cook for 2 hours, or until the beef is very tender. Season with salt and pepper to taste, and serve piping hot.

675g/1¹/₂lb boned and cubed shin of beef

3 large garlic cloves, finely chopped

1 bottle fruity red wine

FROM THE STORECUPBOARD

salt and ground black pepper

VARIATION *Marinate the beef in a mixture of half port and half beef stock instead of the red wine. Port cooks down to produce a lovely rich sauce, but be sure to dilute it with stock because it can be quite overpowering on its own. A half-and-half mixture will give the perfect balance of taste.*

Simple Desserts

WHETHER YOU WANT A REFRESHING AND FRUITY
DESSERT, A DELICIOUS PASTRY TO ENJOY WITH COFFEE
OR AN INDULGENT CREAMY RASPBERRY BRÛLÉE,
SOMETIMES ONLY SOMETHING SWEET WILL DO. THIS
CHAPTER IS PACKED WITH LOVELY IDEAS TO TANTALIZE
THE TASTEBUDS. WHEN DESSERT-MAKING IS THIS
SIMPLE, WHY MAKE DO WITH READY-MADE DESSERTS?
MAKE YOUR OWN AND REALLY ENJOY THE PLEASURE OF
A HOME-MADE TREAT.

Pistachio and Rose Water Oranges

This light and citrusy dessert is perfect to serve after a heavy main course, such as a hearty meat stew or a leg of roast lamb. Combining three favourite Middle Eastern ingredients, it is delightfully fragrant and refreshing. If you don't have pistachio nuts, use hazelnuts instead.

SERVES FOUR

1 Slice the top and bottom off one of the oranges to expose the flesh. Using a small serrated knife, slice down between the pith and the flesh, working round the orange, to remove all the peel and pith. Slice the orange into six rounds, reserving any juice. Repeat with the remaining oranges.

2 Arrange the orange rounds on a serving dish. Mix the reserved juice with the rose water and drizzle over the oranges. Cover the dish with clear film (plastic wrap) and chill for about 30 minutes. Sprinkle the chopped pistachio nuts over the oranges to serve.

4 large oranges

30ml/2 tbsp rose water

30ml/2 tbsp shelled pistachio nuts, roughly chopped

COOK'S TIP
Rose-scented sugar is delicious sprinkled over fresh fruit salads. Wash and thoroughly dry a handful of rose petals and place in a sealed container filled with caster (superfine) sugar for 2–3 days. Remove the petals before using the sugar.

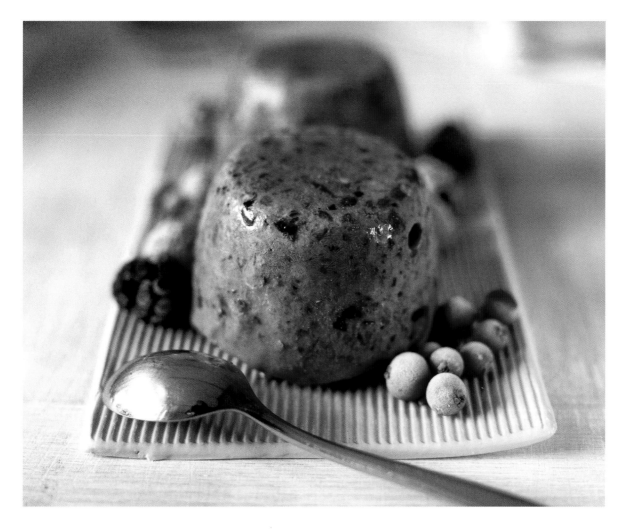

Summer Berry Frozen Yogurt

Any combination of summer fruits will work for this dish, as long as they are frozen, because this helps to create a chunky texture. Whole fresh or frozen berries make an attractive decoration.

SERVES SIX

350g/12oz/3 cups frozen summer fruits

200g/7oz/scant 1 cup Greek (US strained plain) yogurt

25g/1oz icing (confectioners') sugar

VARIATION *To make a rich and creamy ice cream, use double (heavy) cream in place of the yogurt. It's a lot less healthy but the taste is irresistible.*

1 Put all the ingredients into a food processor and process until combined but still quite chunky. Spoon the mixture into six 150ml/¼ pint/⅔ cup ramekin dishes.

2 Cover each dish with clear film (plastic wrap) and place in the freezer for about 2 hours, or until firm.

3 To turn out the frozen yogurts, dip the dishes briefly in hot water and invert them on to small serving plates. Tap the base of the dishes and the yogurts should come out. Serve immediately.

Raspberry Sherbet

Traditional sherbets are made in a similar way to sorbets but with added milk. This low-fat version is made from raspberry purée blended with sugar syrup and virtually fat-free fromage frais or yogurt.

SERVES SIX

175g/6oz/scant 1 cup caster (superfine) sugar

500g/1¼lb/3½ cups raspberries, plus extra, to serve

500ml/17fl oz/2 ¼ cups virtually fat-free fromage frais or yogurt

COOK'S TIP *To make the sherbet by hand, pour the raspberry purée into a freezerproof container and freeze for 4 hours, beating once with a fork, electric whisk or in a food processor to break up the ice crystals. Freeze, then beat again.*

1 Put the sugar in a small pan with 150ml/¼ pint/⅔ cup water and bring to the boil, stirring until the sugar has dissolved completely. Pour into a jug (pitcher) and cool.

2 Put 350g/12oz/2½ cups of the raspberries in a food processor and blend to a purée. Press through a sieve into a large bowl and discard the seeds. Stir the sugar syrup into the raspberry purée and chill until very cold.

3 Add the fromage frais or yogurt to the chilled purée and whisk until smooth. Using an ice-cream maker, churn the mixture until it is thick but too soft to scoop. Scrape into a freezerproof container, then crush the remaining raspberries between your fingers and add to the ice cream. Mix lightly then freeze for 2–3 hours until firm. Scoop the ice cream into dishes and serve with extra raspberries.

Pineapple Crush Ice Cream

Look out for pineapples that are labelled "extra sweet". This variety has bright sunflower-yellow flesh that is naturally sweet and juicy. It is ideal for making the most wonderful ice cream.

SERVES FOUR TO SIX

1 Slice one pineapple in half lengthwise through the leafy top, then scoop out the flesh from both halves, keeping the shells intact. Stand them upside down to drain, wrap in clear film (plastic wrap) and chill until needed.

2 Trim the top off the remaining pineapple, cut the flesh into slices, then cut away the skin and any eyes. Remove the core from each slice, then finely chop the flesh from both pineapples. Purée 300g/11oz of the pineapple in a food processor or blender, reserving the remaining pineapple.

3 Using an ice-cream maker, churn the pineapple purée with the sugar for 15–20 minutes. Mix in the cream and churn until thick but too soft to scoop.

4 Add 175g/6oz/1¹/₂ cups of the pineapple and continue to churn the ice cream until it is stiff enough to serve in scoops. Serve, offering any remaining pineapple separately.

2 extra-sweet pineapples

50g/2oz/¹/₄ cup caster (superfine) sugar

300ml/¹/₂ pint/1¹/₄ cups whipping cream

VARIATION *This ice cream is also delicious mixed with meringues: crumble four meringue nests into the ice cream mixture when adding the pineapple.*

Chocolate Banana Fools

This de luxe version of banana custard looks great served in glasses. It can be made a few hours in advance and chilled until ready to serve.

SERVES FOUR

1 Put the chocolate in a heatproof bowl and melt in the microwave on high power for 1–2 minutes. Stir, then set aside to cool. (Alternatively, put the chocolate in a heatproof bowl and place it over a pan of gently simmering water and leave until melted, stirring frequently.)

2 Pour the custard into a bowl and gently fold in the melted chocolate to make a rippled effect.

3 Peel and slice the bananas and stir these into the chocolate and custard mixture. Spoon into four glasses and chill for 30 minutes–1 hour before serving.

115g/4oz plain (semisweet) chocolate, chopped

300ml/¹/₂ pint/1¹/₄ cups fresh custard

2 bananas

Lemon Posset

This simple creamy dessert has distant origins, dating back to the Middle Ages. It is perfect for warm summer evenings and is particularly good served with crisp shortbread cookies.

SERVES FOUR

1 Gently heat the cream and sugar together until the sugar has dissolved, then bring to the boil, stirring constantly. Add the lemon juice and rind and stir until the mixture thickens.

2 Pour the mixture into four heatproof serving glasses and chill until just set, then serve.

600ml/1 pint/2¹/₂ cups double (heavy) cream

175g/6oz/scant 1 cup caster (superfine) sugar

grated rind and juice of 2 unwaxed lemons

COOK'S TIP *To make shortbread cookies, put 225g/8oz/1 cup chilled butter in a food processor and add 115g/4oz/²/₃ cup caster (superfine) sugar, 225g/8oz/2 cups plain (all-purpose) flour and 115g/4oz/²/₃ cup ground rice. Process to form a dough, then shape into a log 5cm/2in wide and wrap in clear film (plastic wrap). Chill for 30 minutes. Preheat the oven to 190°C/375°F/Gas 5. Cut the dough into thin slices, and bake for 15–20 minutes.*

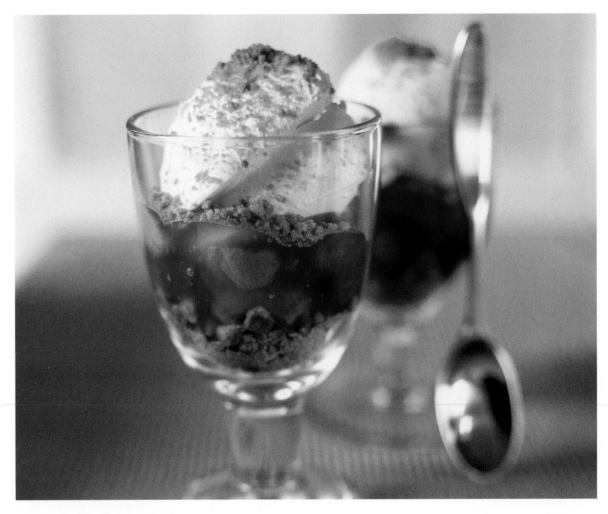

Rhubarb and Ginger Trifles

Choose a good quality jar of rhubarb compote for this recipe; try to find one with large, chunky pieces of fruit.

SERVES FOUR

**12 gingernut biscuits
(gingersnaps)**

**50ml/2fl oz/¹/₄ cup rhubarb
compote**

**450ml/³/₄ pint/scant 2 cups
extra thick double (heavy)
cream**

1 Put the ginger biscuits in a plastic bag and seal. Bash the biscuits with a rolling pin until roughly crushed.

2 Set aside two tablespoons of crushed biscuits and divide the rest among four glasses.

3 Spoon the rhubarb compote on top of the crushed biscuits, then top with the cream. Place in the refrigerator and chill for about 30 minutes.

4 To serve, sprinkle the reserved crushed biscuits over the trifles and serve immediately.

Strawberry Cream Shortbreads

These pretty desserts are always popular. Serve them as soon as they are ready because the shortbread cookies will lose their lovely crisp texture if left to stand.

SERVES THREE

150g/5oz strawberries

450ml/³/₄ pint/scant 2 cups double (heavy) cream

6 round shortbread biscuits (cookies)

VARIATION

You can use any other berry you like for this dessert – try raspberries or blueberries. Two ripe, peeled peaches will also give great results.

1 Reserve three strawberries for decoration. Hull the remaining strawberries and cut them in half.

2 Put the halved strawberries in a bowl and gently crush using the back of a fork. (Only crush the berries lightly; they should not be reduced to a purée.)

3 Put the cream in a large, clean bowl and whip to form soft peaks. Add the crushed strawberries and gently fold in to combine. (Do not overmix.)

4 Halve the reserved strawberries, then spoon the strawberry and cream mixture on top of the shortbread cookies. Decorate each one with half a strawberry and serve immediately.

Raspberry Brûlée

Cracking through the caramelized sugary top of a crème brûlée to reveal the creamy custard underneath is always so satisfying. These ones have the added bonus of a deliciously rich, fruity custard packed with crushed raspberries.

SERVES FOUR

1 Tip the raspberries into a large bowl and crush with a fork. Add the custard and gently fold in until combined.

2 Divide the mixture between four 120ml/4fl oz/¹/₂ cup ramekin dishes. Cover each one with clear film (plastic wrap) and chill in the refrigerator for 2–3 hours.

3 Preheat the grill (broiler) to high. Remove the clear film from the ramekin dishes and place them on a baking sheet. Sprinkle the sugar over the custards and grill (broil) for 3–4 minutes, or until the sugar has caramelized.

4 Remove the custards from the grill and set aside for a few minutes to allow the sugar to harden, then serve.

115g/4oz fresh raspberries

300ml/¹/₂ pint/1¹/₄ cups ready-made fresh custard

75g/3oz caster (superfine) sugar

COOK'S TIP *You can now buy little gas blow torches for use in the kitchen. They make quick work of caramelizing the sugar on top of the brûlées – and are also fun to use!*

Portuguese Custard Tarts

Called *pastéis de nata* in Portugal, these tarts are traditionally served with a small strong coffee as a sweet breakfast dish, but they are equally delicious served as a pastry or dessert.

MAKES TWELVE

225g/8oz ready-made puff pastry, thawed if frozen

175ml/6fl oz/³/₄ cup fresh ready-made custard

30ml/2 tbsp icing (confectioners') sugar

1 Preheat the oven to 200°C/400°F/Gas 6. Roll out the pastry and cut out twelve 13cm/5in rounds. Line a 12-hole muffin tin (pan) with the pastry rounds. Line each pastry round with a circle of baking parchment and some baking beans or uncooked rice.

2 Bake the tarts for 10–15 minutes, or until the pastry is cooked through and golden. Remove the paper and baking beans or rice and set aside to cool.

3 Spoon the custard into the pastry cases and dust with the icing sugar. Place the tarts under a preheated hot grill (broiler) and cook until the sugar caramelizes. Remove from the heat and leave to cool before serving.

Plum and Almond Tart

To transform this tart into an extravagant dessert, dust with a little icing (confectioners') sugar and serve with a dollop of crème fraîche.

SERVES FOUR

1 Preheat the oven to 190°C/375°F/Gas 5. Unroll the pastry on to a large baking sheet. Using a small, sharp knife, score a border 5cm/2in from the edge of the pastry, without cutting all the way through.

2 Roll out the marzipan into a rectangle, to fit just within the pastry border, then lay it on top of the pastry, pressing down lightly with the tips of your fingers.

3 Scatter the sliced plums on top of the marzipan in an even layer and bake for 20–25 minutes, or until the pastry is risen and golden brown.

4 Carefully transfer the tart to a wire rack to cool slightly, then cut into squares or wedges and serve.

375g/13oz ready-rolled puff pastry, thawed if frozen

115g/4oz marzipan

6–8 plums, stoned and sliced

Baked Apples with Marsala

The Marsala cooks down with the juice from the apples and the butter to make a rich, sticky sauce. Serve these delicious apples with a spoonful of extra-thick cream.

SERVES SIX

1 Preheat the oven to 180°C/350°F/Gas 4. Using an apple corer, remove the cores from the apples and discard.

2 Place the apples in a small, shallow baking pan and stuff the figs into the holes in the centre of each apple.

3 Top each apple with a quarter of the butter and pour over the Marsala. Cover the pan tightly with foil and bake for about 30 minutes.

4 Remove the foil from the apples and bake for a further 10 minutes, or until the apples are tender and the juices have reduced slightly. Serve immediately with any remaining pan juices drizzled over the top.

4 medium cooking apples

50g/2oz/¹/₃ cup ready-to-eat dried figs

150ml/¹/₄ pint/²/₃ cup Marsala

FROM THE STORECUPBOARD

50g/2oz/¹/₄ cup butter, softened

Damson Water Ice

Perfectly ripe damsons are sharp and full of flavour – if you can't find damsons, use another deep-red variety of plum or extra-juicy Victoria plums. To add an extra, nutty flavour to this mouthwatering ice, serve sprinkled with finely chopped toasted almonds.

SERVES SIX

500g/1¼lb ripe damsons, washed

150g/5oz/¾ cup caster (superfine) sugar

1 Put the damsons into a pan and add 150ml/¼ pint/⅔ cup water. Cover and simmer gently for 10 minutes, or until the damsons are tender.

2 Pour 300ml/½ pint/1¼ cups water into a second pan. Add the sugar and bring to the boil, stirring until the sugar has dissolved. Pour the syrup into a bowl, leave to cool, then chill.

3 Break up the cooked damsons in the pan with a wooden spoon and scoop out any free stones (pits). Pour the fruit and juices into a large sieve set over a bowl. Press the fruit through the sieve and discard the skins and any remaining stones from the sieve.

4 Pour the damson purée into a shallow plastic container. Stir in the syrup and freeze for 6 hours, beating once or twice to break up the ice crystals.

5 Spoon into tall serving glasses or dishes and serve the water ice with wafers.

VARIATION *Apricot water ice can be made in exactly the same way. Flavour the water ice with a little lemon or orange rind or add a broken cinnamon stick to the pan when poaching the fruit. Serve garnished with sprigs of mint or nasturtium flowers.*

Index